Art & Soul

Art & Soul

Poems by

Barbara Lydecker Crane

© 2025 Barbara Lydecker Crane. All rights reserved.
This material may not be reproduced in any form, published,
reprinted, recorded, performed, broadcast,
rewritten or redistributed without
the explicit permission of Barbara Lydecker Crane.
All such actions are strictly prohibited by law.

Cover design by Shay Culligan
Cover image by Shutterstock
Author photo by Sarah O'Neill

ISBN: 978-1-63980-923-3

Kelsay Books
502 South 1040 East, A-119
American Fork, Utah 84003
Kelsaybooks.com

Acknowledgments

I am grateful to the following publications, who first published these poems (many in slightly different forms):

Alabama Literary Review: "Shoes on the Danube Promenade," "The Resplendent Quetzal"
America: "March 21st"
American Arts Quarterly: "Portrait of the Artist" (with title "Portrait of the Artist as an Old Man")
Amethyst Review: "High Commission"
Angle: "Meeting St. Malo"
Ars Medica: "The Invaders"
Autumn Sky Poetry Daily: "At a Cemetery Door"
Blue Unicorn: "What You Seek Is Seeking You," "Courtly Dance" (with title "Swan Villanelle"), "The Real Thing," "Old Irish Superstitions"
Ekphrastic Review: "Masterwork"
First Things: "Sides of Pride"
The Ghazal Page: "Finding Rumi in a Wine Bar," "It"
Innisfree Poetry Journal: "Handsome Mares"
Light: "My Letter to Sonnet Insurance" (with title "Sonnet Insurance")
Lucid Rhythms: "Guided Hike at the Volcano" (with title "Guide to the Volcano")
Maria Faust Sonnet Contest (webpage): "Paradise Leased" (as a 2018 Laureate's Choice winner)
Measure: "Shards of Knowing"
Mezzo Cammin: "Begin Again," "Once"
New Verse Review: "Reverberations"
Old Frog Pond: "Emergence"
The Orchards Poetry Journal: "Spiral"

Panoply: "My Block of Time"
Poemeleon: "Yours in Faith, Aaron Bride"
Poetry by the Sea (webpage): "Roughly True" (as 2024 winner, Sonnet Crown category, Kim Bridgford Memorial Sonnet Contest)
Pulsebeat: "Perhaps," "A Turn of Events"
Rattle: "Love Refrains" (as a 2017 Rattle Poetry Prize finalist)
Sonnet Scroll: "Grinnell Glacier Drawings"
THINK: A Journal of Poetry, Fiction, and Essays: "Encountering Escher" (with title "Generation"), "Gallarus Oratory," "Flying" (with title "Harbinger"), "Hearing *Fado* in Lisbon," "Naming the Sacred," "Since My Father's Death," "The Stone Carver"
14 x 14: "Garden Wedding"

Honors which did not include publication:

2024 Frost Farm Prize, Honorable Mention: "Icons"
2011 Helen Schaible Sonnet Contest, First Prize: "Yours in Faith, Aaron Brede"

Other Books by Barbara Lydecker Crane

You Will Remember Me (ekphrastic sonnets and art reproductions, Able Muse Press, 2023)

BackWords Logic (humor, with drawings by Frances McCormick, Local Gems Press, 2017)

Alphabetricks (for children, Kelsay Books, 2013)

Zero Gravitas (humor, Kelsay Books, 2012)

Contents

Once	15
At a Cemetery Door	16
Love Refrains	17
Sides of Pride	18
Grinnell Glacier Drawings	19
Encountering Escher	20
The Stone Carver	21
Begin Again	23
A Portrait of the Artist	25
Meeting Saint Malo	26
Finding Rumi in a Wine Bar	27
What You Seek Is Seeking You	28
Intrigue at the Abbey	29
High Commission	36
Masterwork	37
It	38
Emergence	40
A Mirror of Swallows	41
Courtly Dance	42
The Real Thing	43
Yours in Faith, Aaron Brede	44
Hearing Fado Music in Lisbon	45
One Roman Shoe	46
Beloved	47
Perhaps	48
Roughly True	49
Shoes on the Danube Promenade	53
A Turn of Events	54
Reverberations	55
Church Bells of Italy	58
Montmartre	59

Handsome Mares	60
Drive to Write	61
My Letter to Sonnet Insurance	62
Taking My Measure	63
Flying	66
The Invaders	67
My Block of Time	68
Old Irish Superstitions	69
Gallarus Oratory	70
Shards of Knowing	71
Garden Wedding	74
Since My Father's Death	75
Icons	76
Guided Hike at the Volcano	77
Namaste	79
Bring no harm to the trees . . .	80
Paradise Leased	82
March 21st	83
Spiral	84
The Resplendent Quetzal	85
Naming the Sacred	86

Once

We gently blew each liquid sphere
into a galaxy of single, double
planets through the branches. Sheer

membranes meeting roughened bark,
we gaped to see, clung to stubble.
The air was sodden in the park,

each twig a dark, accusing finger.
That morning had portended trouble,
but now we watched enchantment linger.

The dogwood shimmered with a trim
of iridescence made of bubble.
We children circled in a rim

for time untold until at last
magic popped into a puddle
and entered, as it must, the past.

At a Cemetery Door

Dad gave me permission to explore
the other graves while he sat down to rest
at Grandpa's. Shedding Sunday shoes I wore,

I searched for recent dates, short spans—my test
designed to prove that modern-day children
rarely die. My census brought success.

Then at a tiny house of stone, my skin
prickled as I peered beyond the glass door.
I shrieked to glimpse the vision just within—

two small pale feet faced me on that floor.
I jumped back and leapt through cold, wet grass
to blurt to Dad the sight I'd seen. He roared

with laughter, mocking my forgetting that glass
reflects the looker. "Of course!" I piped, and tried
to laugh to let the haunting image pass.

Yet I could see my cold white feet inside
a tomb in a chain of days or decades more,
and that new vision could not be denied.

Love Refrains

Mom banged her hairbrush down in a reprimand of love.
"What an awful question! You don't understand love.

"Of course Dad loves you. How can you question that?
He doesn't have to blare it out, like a brass band of love.

"You aren't a princess to be coddled on a lap or praised
without good reason. That's a never-never land of love.

"Your father works hard, with a great deal on his mind.
Now don't go causing trouble, making a demand of love.

"Yes, I know he yells and sends you to your room a lot.
But be glad he never hits you with the backhand of love.

"Once, banished to your room, you drew a picture poem
for him. I watched him beam at you with unplanned love.

"He said he's proud of you. I've heard him tell you twice."
She brushed my hair, hard. "Barbara, that's a brand of love."

Sides of Pride

Trouble lies in feeling proud.
I was taught that it's a sin
and that I shouldn't share aloud

some gift with which I was endowed.
My gloating crow and Cheshire grin
burst that bubble, feeling proud.

Bragging rights? My friends weren't wowed;
I lost a few. I couldn't win.
Better not to share aloud,

deflect my gifts amid the crowd.
But self-effacement wears me thin.
It's trouble, a lie, to *not* feel proud.

There's joy in peeking through a cloud
and beaming, now and then, to kin.
I will choose to share aloud

a well-earned pride to those avowed
by ties of birth or love within
and double down on feeling proud—
it's blissful sin when shared aloud.

Grinnell Glacier Drawings

These drawings aren't from life. I wasn't there;
the others kept on hiking to the glacier.
Beside the lake I perched on my fold-up chair,
sketchbook spread across my lap. Erasures
of errant starts scratched into the page,
like tiny echoes of the creeping scrape
of ice and stone in the last glacial age.
Rock striations—every shadow and shape—
kept shifting in the light. I let it fall,
my book, and closed my eyes.
                                Then, two times,
I startled at a distant, feral call,
a minor-key lament that dipped and climbed,
recording into bedrock memory
these views that I imagined I could see.

Encountering Escher

Day and Night, 1938, woodcut by M.C. Escher, Netherlands

A river arcs away in brilliant light
and returns in mirror image, inky black.
The artist's knife has carved a day to night
that flickers faster than my eyes can track.
The foreground holds some patchwork, furrowed fields,
squares that bend and fall away, transmute
into the most astonishing of yields—
geese, flying left and right. It's absolute
alchemy.
         I study changes row by row—
how birds emerge, articulating wings
in tessellating shapes. The more I know,
the more I marvel: life so lightly springs
and fills the air above the towns and farms
held between this pair of river arms.

The Stone Carver

> *Untitled*, c.1960s, stone sculpture by an unnamed
> Inuit artist (Northwest Territories, Canada)

I will not sign my name to this piece of stone,
though I'll keep on carving a creature like a bird
in gray-green serpentine. On nearby Baffin Island
I quarry a sackful each summer, my knobby hands
cracking a hammer and wedge on the wall of rock.
I roughed a bird's head first, then the neck's curve,

imagining a loon—afloat, alert. But now the curve
of serpentine seems to birth the body of a seal. Stone
strata low on its back ripple like black water rocking
when a seal bobs up a breathing hole, or when a bird
splashes down. All sea creatures are fingers on the hand
of Sedna, the sea spirit surrounding our Inuit islands.

My mother, Aya, sang to Sedna on our little island,
Qaummaarviit, "the place that shines." Warm, that curve
of Aya's back, as we slept under skins. Father Etuk's hands
were stained with walrus blood. With eyes steady as stones,
he'd carve from tusks. His little walrus sits above the bird-
seal on my bench, to oversee my carving of these rocks.

When Etuk died, Aya tucked me in her anorak and rocked
me as she wept and walked. Sharp cries sliced the island's
bright blue air—terns, coots, plovers—all our summer birds
who fly up here to breed. Once I spied the shining curve
of a snow goose egg nestled in the grass. Cold as stone,
I remember that white world in my small, cupped hands.

Did we eat that egg? Too long ago . . . and now my hands
ache. It's late. I step out to the dark and wince at "rock
and roll" pulsing the new community hall. Slapping stone
dust off my arms, I gaze at the Aurora glow up-island—
swirl of violet, billow of green, shiver of white like curving
fringe on Aya's dancing skirt. Sky Aya rustles like a bird

in her nest. Turquoise spreads like wings of a great bird—
a harbinger of spring? I answer, singing low, till icy hands
and feet drive me back inside warm walls. Jagged curves
await my hours of sanding down this changeling rock.
I'll sell it to the agent when he comes. Far from this island,
city galleries tout "Eskimo Art Carved from Native Stone."

On the bottom of this stone, this green creature of Sedna's hand
and mine, I'll etch an outline of a bird-shaped island, and around
its rocky curve, my government-issued artist's number. My seal.

Begin Again

Begin again. A length of palest blue,
horizon for a landscape quilt, might do.
Walk outdoors at dawn and breathe the view

of birches and the bay. Begin again
to step outside the frozen time; mend
the empty morning with your eyes and hands.

You blend a sky till you bemoan your old
imitation of the gray-blue glow
that melds itself to green and then to gold.

Go on. Begin again with lime and leaf
and darker ivy—living greens in cloth
for sunlit lawn and shadows from the sheaf

of trees. Begin again with scraps. By chance
you cobble up the birches' texture. Branches
sway and trunks bow in an ancient dance,

a harmony you long to join again.
The shadows of the birch trees can extend
in gauzy strips. But as you cut and pin,

once more you stop and wince. It won't be caught,
your vision. It makes you want to pull your hair out!
Do it. Pluck a strand—just one, and thread it—

begin again as sparrows stitch the air
with music. Ply your needle now with care;
it whispers through a patch of sky. There,

at last, a new creation will begin:
the wings of your dragonfly are glinting
in the sun. This work is from within.

A Portrait of the Artist

You tell yourself you're good at what you do,
at least according to your friends and those
who've credited your artwork in review.
Portrait painting decades now, you chose
this work (which even then was out of fashion)
because each likeness you could bring alive
would spur you to another. But now your passion
ebbs, as restlessness and age connive.
Why don't you close your eyes to see in dreams
another pastime you once found enthralling?
Step outside the gilded frame that seems
to hold you flat, and take this as your calling:
enliven years of time's diminishing
with challenges a change of work can bring.

Meeting Saint Malo

Saint Malo, 13th c., limestone sculpture
by an unnamed artist, France

Ennui and I had wandered every wing
before I ambled into one room more—
Medieval Reliquaries, where now I creak
in desultory solitude. I groan
at the sound of children in encroaching roar,

and turn to leave. But then a statue brings
my second look and longer gaze. For sure,
it's no Adonis, and yet the visage speaks
with an impish little grin carved in stone,
this *Saint Malo,* small fisherman on shore.

I picture how he'd cast a net of string
beyond his bobbing wooden boat's oars.
I picture he'd just chuckle when a sleek
mackerel leapt his grasp. In baritone,
I hear him sing for all that he adored.

The statue's signage tells a startling thing:
It's said that Malo walked on water. What lore—
this simple soul, transcendent and unique!
In my transcending dreams, I skate alone
on the moonlit mirror of a pond, or soar

over it with whistling swans in spring.
But who can walk on water? What could afford
this power to him of human, slight physique?
Perhaps a buoyant spirit all his own.
I'm whistling now, and flying out the door.

Finding Rumi in a Wine Bar

> Rumi was a 13th c. Persian mystic, scholar, philosopher, and poet.
> His quoted words (some paraphrased here) are from *The Essential
> Rumi,* translations by Coleman Barks with John Moyne.

With wine to wet his thirsty lips, mystic Rumi never runs out
of words: "Loosen your tongue; don't worry what comes out."

He wiggles his fingers in the air. "Don't hand me another glass.
Just pour it in my mouth." I do, and then the man hums out,

"Having nothing produces provisions." If only he would give
a hint of how to net a harvest when the tide of income's out.

Rumi talks of emptiness, patience, and whirling while one waits:
"Dance, when broken open." Distant lute music now strums out.

He smiles as he recounts how joy may often eclipse dismay.
"The prophet Muhammad, cooling his bare feet, felt plumb out

of luck when an eagle plucked one of his boots and flew off.
In that bird's beak, the boot turned—and what tumbled out?

"A poisonous snake! God brings us disappointment to avert
a greater disaster." Not all reason's in our grasp. Some's out.

What You Seek Is Seeking You

—often attributed to Rumi

Praise elates me on the phone,
that message left in baritone.

Something's rattling at my door . . .
inspiration evermore?

Confidence that takes a bow
is striding up before me now.

It draws me into its embrace.
I've been found! I rest my chase.

Intrigue at the Abbey

A tale in seven voices, c.1500, Paris

I. Brother Bernard, abbot:

"Even before this crime, we hardly thrived.
Demand for manuscripts had greatly waned
as printing presses started to arrive.
A scribe, an artist, a helper—just those remained,
along with one corrector. With luck I landed
an order for a lavish Book of Hours
of prayers, psalms, and gilded art. To be candid,
this plum was won by fawning to the power
of an older silk merchant of high station:
*Your new young bride deserves the very best
of script, art, and gold illumination,*
I wheedled. He agreed and left the rest
to me. But now my voice begins to fail.
I'll let the others tell the grievous tale."

II. Brother Jerome, scribe:

"It takes a year, a Book of Hours jewel,
and we had just four months to toil in.
I set to work, incising every rule
before I penned my Roundhand letters, akin
to choristers with curving backs in rows
(so different from the older Gothic style
of script, with pointy knees and jabbing elbows).
My own bony body posed a trial
daily at my bench. But with a new
quill pen, a flight feather of a swan,
then through the church's calendar I flew—
through saints' and feast days my letters hurried on.
I left blank the highest holidays:
in brilliant red, those words would later blaze."

III. Marguerite, itinerant rubricator*:

"I begged the monk who peered around the door,
I'm sore in need of work, with doleful eyes.
I bring my father's quills and inks (the more
I spoke, the less I quavered in my lies);
last month he sadly perished of La Peste.**
In welcome warmth I then was shown a seat,
and on a scrap of parchment with my best
red ink, I penned my test: *Je suis Marguerite.*
A serif capped my J; my M stood twined
in vine. With widened eyes, that monk asked
if I might start at once. Another was kind
and found a guesthouse nook for me. A task
for pay . . . a warm, safe place to sleep, be fed . . .
I put aside my qualms, and laid my head."

IV. Brother Lucien, illuminator:

"What I bring to a book is precious light.
Is not my name an aptly given one?
Each saint and maid I paint, each upright knight,
reflects my gift—this godly benison.
I've drawn Saint George astride his bridled steed,
his lance upraised to strike a fatal blow
to the wounded dragon below. To watch his deed,
I'm adding in this distant girl, aglow
in ginger hair like Marguerite's—it strays
from out her wimple. That old bird Jerome
is quick these winter days to warm with praise
for how she scribes beyond her monochrome.
She intrigues us all. I overheard
her laughing with Emil, and I was stirred."

V. Emil, illuminator's helper:

"Those mingy monks paid less in francs than prayers.
Good-for-naught, such words for me. I mixed
the powders for Lucien's pigments, well aware
of arsenic and mercury I fixed
in emerald green, vermillion, aster yellow.
It fell to me to add the dung or piss,
the agents making all the dye pots mellow.
Lucien never saw the alchemist
in me, though I could raise a rose from dust.
He never let me lift a brush to paint,
although I begged. Behind his back I cussed.
But to that redhead scribe I was a saint.
She knew the piddling coins that I was paid—
I gave some to that wily, willing maid."

VI. Brother Godfrey, corrector:

"The scribes would pass each lettered page to me
and I'd peruse it, penknife in my hand.
I'd scrape mistakes in psalms and litanies
and prayers (all at my memory's command).
My blade would cleanse each sin—every error—
be it of commission or omission.
Bernard was pacing round the room in terror
of late delivery to his patrician.
Jerome, intent on pages to revise,
was working close beside that comely female.
Emil's eyes on her made me surmise
some sort of dalliance. I espied a trail
of daisy petals underfoot—discreet
signals, perhaps, strewn in marguerites."

VII. Simon, a Paris bookbinder:

"When old Bernard burst in my shop, I steeled
my nerve. That abbot spluttered, face beet-red,
Marguerite has fled with young Emil—
they stole our gold! He shook his tonsured head
and proffered me a parcel. *Thank heaven*
they did not pilfer this. How many days
to stitch and bind these precious pages? 'Seven,'
I professed, and hoped his rheumy gaze
would miss the flecks that glinted on my floor
and the hairs on my chemise like threads of red.
With gold and pages, we three will flee before
cockcrow. Bustling Antwerp lies ahead.
we'll purchase what the future will be told in:
a printing press. Our business will be golden."

*v. III: Rubrication was the use of red ink for headings, high holidays and important text sections in manuscripts.
**v. III: La Peste was a French name for bubonic plague.

High Commission

Christ of the Deesis, c.1260, wall mosaic
by an unnamed artist, Hagia Sophia, Istanbul

My workers toiled for their meager pay.
They chiseled glass and stone, mixed grout, and set in
just an inch of my design each day.
These bits of beveled, colored glass let in
a presence brought to life by changing light.
They're set atilt, in order to reflect
the glimmers of both sun and lamplit night,
and lend a mystic, heavenly effect.
My tiled Jesus stands with right hand lifted
to judge how worthy each of us has been.
Artistic bent does not mean I am gifted,
but art is what I give to God and men.
Earthly Emperor, this work is now complete.
Heavenly King, judge kindly when we meet.

Masterwork

frescoes by Michelangelo, 1508-1512,
Sistine Chapel, Italy

It's done at last. My back and neck complain
from four full years of working under strain.
I climbed on scaffolds where I had to crane
my neck to paint the vaulted, vast domain.
Assistants were inept and proved a bane;
I was the only one who could sustain
the vision and the toil and the pain
to bring to life the sacred and profane
mass of figures the ceiling would contain.
There God and Adam, at the center, reign;
I painted God as father—kind, humane—
as he imparts the spark of heart and brain
to Adam. God gives us all free will, free rein
to set our sights, to struggle, and attain.

It

Does the spirit choose me, or must I choose it?
Can a writer curry favor with lines to amuse it?

The batik artist swirls her awe of Northern Lights
in violet and electric blue, dyeing to transfuse it.

Stirring his spirit in bottles and vats, the distiller
pours himself into his life's work and brews it.

The jazz drummer falls into a soulful rhythm,
and on his snare behind the band he tattoos it.

The bank president pursues a soul ownership;
religious interest compounds as he accrues it.

To the cook, soul is just more food for thought.
He salts it away for later and then barbecues it.

When she receives a blessing, the proofreader
always suspects a mistake and must peruse it.

Attacked by a bear, the atheist blurts a prayer,
and then with Herculean effort he subdues it.

Even when it rains one calamity after another,
the faithful elder raises an umbrella to excuse it.

She knows a communion wafer should dissolve
in the mouth, but the impish goddess chews it.

"Impish God eschews it, the truth we seek,"
theologians sigh, however each construes it.

Hasn't this game has gone on long enough?
Seek a higher spirit, Barb—use it or lose It.

Emergence

From specks of eggs inert a year
and forest floors gray-brown and sere,
    beetle legs creep.

Past pebbles ground by sea to sand
and seaweed fronds by current fanned,
    silver scales leap.

Through winds that swell and buffet seas
and April lace of branching trees,
    white wings sweep.

The seasons, sun, and sea are skeins
that weave new life from roots and veins
    and unseen sources deep.

A Mirror of Swallows

They fly
as if on cue;
each outspread wing
beats and then grows still
as swallows swoop, veer, and glide
in a chittering flock, skimming this little kettle pond—
while below, fork-tailed shadows slide
between sun's glints until,
as one, birds upswing
and soar in blue
noon sky.

Courtly Dance

Swans are swaying in a courtship dance
on the inlet shore, a grassy fen—
perhaps in battle, or in fine romance.

Flapping flags of wings, gunning glances
at the other island nation sovereign,
they can't be swaying in a courtship dance.

If she retreats, likely he'll advance.
This land, perhaps, within his ken—
hence, a courthouse battle. Or romance

may make them more than stately confidants.
Liquid necks bend down and back again;
they might be swaying in a courtship dance.

Perhaps she eyes his puffed-up breast askance,
reluctant to demur into amen
to enter battle or a fine romance.

Is there a treaty under mossy plants,
awaiting signing by this cob and pen?
I only know they sway in courtly dance—
perhaps in the battle of a fine romance.

The Real Thing

With rangy limbs and loping walk, the cartwheel of you
turned my head that fall, and I fell for the appeal of you.

Your eyes listened, sparkling in tandem with your smile.
Slow dancing, you'd wrap me in the humming feel of you.

Letter writing kept the bond between us. In black and white
(your cutaway, my gown), I daydreamed a newsreel of you

and me on our wedding day. The year you were in the war
our voice cassettes flew back and forth. The ordeal for you

was to serve; for us, to last. I had an nightmare where you
came back silent, surly, mean. Nightmares, surreal for you,

pictured injury as your last days of duty dwindled to a few.
I barreled to the airport, hands shaking at the wheel till you

bounded out the door. We could not unwrap our arms.
This ring that wraps my finger is the lifetime seal of you.

I squawk and coo to one who's become a hardy old bird,
a white-crowned crane. I pen these lines with zeal for you.

Yours in Faith, Aaron Brede

Ann Lee, known as "Mother Ann," was the founder of the c. 18th–19th Shaker religious communities, which required celibacy.

Dear Mother Ann,
                   I'm writing by the light
of a candle end. The snores of the older men
are sounding round me just like saws tonight,
crosscutting ragged scratchings of my pen.
I've done my best at cutting birch and pine,
at smoothing lath for chairs, at hauling stone
for schoolhouse walls. I know the Lord's design
requires my improvement—I must atone,
and so I miss my rest and write to you.
At meals, at meetings, a dozen times a day,
I spy Eliza. Our faces burn, untrue
to rules. We love the Lord. But as we pray,
our eyes are dancing. Must I leave? She'd
follow. I'd choose Eliza over creed.

Hearing Fado Music in Lisbon

Fado (Portuguese): fate or destiny.

Quivering notes of a throaty soprano
cascade down to a minor key.
The man on guitar strums to follow
her lead; in lush polyphony
      the notes entwine.
      Their bodies incline
to each other in fluid symmetry,
as if consoling for the woe

harbored from so long ago,
that trio of calamities:
earthquake, tidal wave—*cuidado!*—
then fire consuming antiquities.
      Thirty thousand died.
      Those who survived,
with toil, tears, and rosaries,
rebuilt. They widened streets with sorrow.

Songs have wound around this shadow,
mourning blows of history.
Yet they warm as well as harrow:
Fado stirs up fiery,
      instinctive need,
      the urge to feed
the body with close company.
Laments rekindle love in *fado*.

One Roman Shoe

> At Vindolanda, site of a Roman fort in Northumberland, England
> (then known as Brinaich), many leather shoes have been unearthed.

Who might have laced and worn this leather shoe
inside this fort, two thousand years ago?
Perhaps a Roman, both soldier and cobbler, used
the finest cowhide and new designs to show
devotion; he'd cut with care these loops in rows
that rise from toe to top, and finely score
the filigree at ankle. He'd suppose
this artful present would not be ignored,
but he'd be patient. The soldier-cobbler knew—
could not forget—that when his troop invaded
this Brinaich village the year before, they slew
the men and older boys and quickly mated
with the comely women. This man desired
to win the stocky one, with man-sized feet
he did not mind a whit. What he admired
was how she lived a life that seemed complete
beneath the canopy of trees and birds.
He rued his troop's destruction of her tribe,
but couldn't tell her, without the Brinaich words.
He'd call these shoes a gift, not a bribe,
for one who dwelled apart—the strong-willed
daughter of a blameless man he'd killed.

Beloved

Portrait of Winckelmann, 1764, oil painting
by Angelica Kauffman, Switzerland

My parents taught me young to sketch and paint,
play cello, sing, and speak in several tongues.
We roved where Papa's art would pay; among
each country's cognoscenti we'd acquaint
ourselves, and I'd perform. When Mama died,
I'd just turned twelve and was bereft and shattered.
Papa drew me close, and taught what mattered—
portraits that suggest what lies inside.

At twenty-two I painted Johann's gaze
to show his warmth, his charm, and subtle wit.
His feather pen and weighty books befit
his learning. When I spoke my love and praise,
he was kind, but my new grief won't end:
a woman, he said, can only be his friend.

Perhaps

Travesti, undated mixed media by Ghasem Hajizadeh
(b.1947 in Iran, he emigrated to Paris after the 1979
Iranian Revolution)

I worked this piece in oil paint and scraps
of vintage photographs to show, perhaps,
a striking woman dressed to meet a man
and step out for an evening in Tehran;
they'll drink and dine in a smoky cabaret
and dance close as jazz musicians play.
And after? Viewer, that's for you to guess—
or if you are like many, to repress.
You'll note the hands, and feet in red high heels,
are large. That cashmere sweater surely feels
divine, sliding off one shoulder. The chest
beneath is model-slim. To be so dressed
can give some pleasure, and also can evade
arrest—that is, if he is not betrayed.

Roughly True

    Suzanne Valadon (1865–1938), Paris

What, you haven't heard of me, despite
my art and stormy life? There's much to tell
of pride and bitterness, of bliss and hell—
but not regret. I'll fill my pen and write.

I was born a bastard. *Maman* worked,
a laundress, while I'd roam Montmartre, spying
through café and brothel doors, trying
to snitch some fruit or francs. I laughed and lurked.
With lumps of coal I loved to draw on streets.
Ditching convent school at puberty,
I learned to earn my way. I felt so free
in circus work, curvaceous and petite
and daring on the high trapeze, strong
until I hurt my back. I fell headlong.

That set me back, but new work came along—
also daring, deemed risqué—being painted,
a model for men. Few were sainted . . .
nor was I. I didn't think it wrong
to give a man some pleasure and to claim
my own. For one *artiste* I posed unclad
and soon became his favorite lover. I had
his child, and kept my word: I didn't name
that man on papers with a 'Father' line
and kept on working. *Maman* tended him,
my son, Maurice Utrillo—a pseudonym
so he would not be stigmatized by mine,
that of the saucy urchin shedding clothes,
and budding painter, watching men compose.

I watched the colors bloom as men composed.
Toulouse-Lautrec's hues, both somber and bright,
would join or jar to make a mood just right.
He'd talk of wealthy clients and gallery shows
while I could study his techniques with paint.
He studied me and loved my breasts, my hair,
my thighs, my openness to him. I dared
to love that rich midget with no restraint.
When he refused to marry me, my feigned
suicide didn't change his mind.
But what I learned while posing, I combined
with my good eye, instinctive and untrained.
I'd use my wits (and likely my libido)
to paint in oils, with honesty my credo.

I painted nude women by my credo.
When I showed Degas my work, he praised
me with, "Madame, you're one of us!" That raised
my nerve; like those Montmartre men, I'd show
my art—although I wished my name need not
be printed next to 'woman artist,' a tag
suggesting Other like a warning flag.
I'm already Other in my lot
as Bastard-with-a-Bastard history.
Will I be known for art or just my life
of scandal? I never stayed a bourgeois wife,
as two would always tangle into three;
our pacts permitting infidelity
could not prevent one partner's jealousy.

With cryptic music venting jealousy,
Eric Satie was moody, odd, hysteric—
and amusing, in and out of bed. Eric,
like Paul Mousis, loved me zealously,
and it was bound to fray, my double link.
Mousis was rich; Satie holed up in one
squalid room. He slowly came undone
without me to himself—he took to drink
till drink took him. Maurice, by then eighteen,
also drank. As he was prone to rage
and smashing things since an early age,
my mother fed him wine to calm such scenes.
When briefly sober, it was to me he came.
I treasured hearing *Maman* as my name.

Of course Maurice Utrillo made his name
with me his mother-teacher and his Papa
(I tell you now!) Pierre-Auguste Renoir.
Maurice was barely sane, but all the same,
prolific and successful in his art.
His painter colleague André, with brains and flair,
had tireless desire in our affair;
our turbulent trio could not live apart.
With André as our agent, income flowed—
I once took fifty children to the circus . . .
Montmartre beggars crowded round to work us . . .
we'd help out any artist friend who owed.
The stream of money later dried to drought,
but while it flowed I bloomed by giving it out.

Too soon I knew my bloom was giving out—
I missed men's wide-eyed stares, their swiveled heads.
André, still youthful, strayed to other beds;
Maurice would drink or sit around and pout.
We three unraveled into separate ways.
Instead of painting nudes I painted flowers;
they didn't sell but brightened up the hours
of living alone, inviting in malaise,
till I found Gazi. This young, exotic man
takes care of me and listens to my stories,
roughly true—my slights, successes, glories.
I'm seventy-two. I'll end where I began,
a bastard bitch whose art was bold and right.
My pride and grit leave little room for spite.

Shoes on the Danube Promenade

Art installation by Can Togay and Gyula Pauer, 2005, Budapest

Why old-fashioned shoes in rough array
along this high embankment of concrete?
It's as if some families stepped away

to picnic by the river in bare feet,
and afterward they just forgot their shoes.
That daydream, nothing more than self-deceit.

"Iron casts of wartime shoes were fused
to this promenade in memory," then said
the local guide, "of the many hundred Jews

and others rounded up in winter, made to shed
their shoes—for reuse—then shot despite their pleas.
Adults and children fell, bloodied or dead,

to the river below, a frigid forty degrees.
The gunners, Arrow Cross, were local men
who chose to work with occupying Nazis."

In stunned silence I seem to hear again
repeating shots of rifles that delivered
piercing shrieks, dying moans, mayhem.

Beside these pumps and brogues and boots I shiver,
picturing large and little barefoot bodies
floating past and staining red the river.

A Turn of Events

They're long gone, the residents
of the Jewish Quarter, Budapest:
they laid low in World War Two
until they fled or lost their lives.
Then through the Soviet regime,
abandoned homes were left to rack
and ruin. Two generations passed.
Now some enjoy an afterlife.

These "ruin bars" make hip nightlife
for young Hungarians. The blast
of rock music bounces back
from crumbling stucco walls. The gleam
of colored lights enlivens the dives'
decrepitude. Would an old Jew,
returning, run? Or join the rest,
and guzzle beer like recompense?

Reverberations

"I hear an infinite sweetness in the wood,"
a musician said. Ingrained, there is a story
of bitter times that many have withstood.

The epic tale (both truth and allegory)
starts with an African cedar hewn for boards
and crafted to a small, bright-painted dory.

A Libyan fisherman would net rewards
of mackerel, bream, bass, sardines, or hake,
till greater income might not be ignored.

People pay when desperate to make
their way up north to Italy or elsewhere.
Fleeing war or famine, they'll forsake

family, land, language, savings: they're
handing over thousands for the fee
demanded by a boatman. Migrants dare

the crossing of the Mediterranean Sea
although a leaky boat or sudden squall
might spell their end. The only guarantee

is that fear will numb discomfort. All
packed in, chests to backs, seated astride,
most survive. But ruined boats now sprawl

in one Milan empty lot, beside
a crowded, run-down prison. A warden's eyes
envisioned listless inmates occupied

in workshop time reusing wood supplies.
Cedar has a pleasant, spicy smell;
it's easily worked yet durable; it's prized.

A few men were escorted from their cells.
They left the rotting keels like lifeless limbs
but pried some sturdy ribs apart from shells.

Two adept with wood were taught to trim
the boards into surprising shapes anew—
viols', violins', and cellos' slim

ribs, necks, backs, and fronts; they drew
and carved the S-shaped mouths of sound-holes.
The skills and self-esteem of prisoners grew.

"Now I sing with wood," said one who scrolled
a cello front and now would plane and sand.
He'd leave some traces of bright paint, to hold

a deeper sound and memories of the land
of Africa and orange, red, and green
bobbing boats with human contraband.

An orchestra performed with all fourteen
instruments at La Scala opera house,
where their transforming tale was heard and seen

in *The Four Seasons*. What better score to rouse
ovations for redemption and rebirth?
Musicians, inmates, migrants, take your bows!

based on an AP News article in *The Boston Globe,* February 13, 2024

Church Bells of Italy

Through dusky lanes, now comes the peal
of bells that sound their evening chime.
I too am struck, then stilled, to feel
their harmony as tolled notes climb
and dip; they shape an aural keel
for balance through this anxious time.
Three times a day the bells appeal.
Their call might be to One sublime—
and too, to one like me. I heal
my spirit with the music's rhyme.

Montmartre

The Old Guitarist, 1903, oil painting
by Pablo Picasso, France

I slept by day and worked by night. The years
I lived with Carlos in that studio, learning
how to paint, Montmartre filled our ears
and eyes but not our pockets. We were burning
our art for warmth, and overpainting works
to save on canvas. Here, in midnight blue,
a wraith plays his guitar, and Germaine lurks
beneath—the model Carlos loved. I drew
her, then painted over his would-be fiancée.
When she refused his offers and ignored
him, Carlos shot himself. Let me convey
the crippling, cold despair that can be stored
inside. My painted man's guitar, like art,
lets out the lamentations of the heart.

Handsome Mares

The Horse Fair, 1852–55, oil painting
by Rosa Bonheur, France

Breathe in, and you might catch a whiff of dung
in the Paris breeze that's ruffling trees and manes.
This equine pack at market runs high-strung,
resisting muscled men with handlers' reins.
One pair of pearly mares—tails braided, bound—
flash sunlit, dappled flanks in matching pace.
As scores of hoofbeats gallop hardened ground,
do you feel your heart begin to race?
My heart beats best whenever I am sketching
creatures live or dead. In abattoirs
you'd never pick me out; I'm hardly fetching
in men's old clothes and hat, with lit cigar
(for camouflage, not yen to be a male—
I'd sooner be a horse). End of tale.

Drive to Write

Would I could relax and be a passenger in the process.
But at my desk, seat belt fastened, I choose to drive.

The computer teems with distractions—email, games,
Facebook, Instagram—schemes that defuse my drive.

I write, revise, cut and paste. Delete, delete, delete.
So many tone-deaf words put the blues in my drive.

I fetch a snack and scan the threatening summer sky;
keeping a weather eye is another way I lose my drive.

Back at my desk again, I fish through the thesaurus
to recast my lines. New verbs might enthuse my drive.

When thunder rumbles my brain blinks like lightning.
I'm recharged; the perfect phrase renews my drive.

One word leads to another. If I take my time, I might
just write a brilliant book! (Please excuse my drive.)

Would that a mythic guide was idling in a limo, pickup,
or crane outside. Does anyone have a muse to drive?

My Letter to Sonnet Insurance

    company name on a Toronto billboard

Dear Sonnet staff:
                I'm eager for your plan.
I'll want an underwriter old-school-based,
classic but not Jurassic in his taste—
he'd speak my terms. I'd benefit from your man
adjusting rhymes, making meter strict,
and assuming the risk of an errant anapest.
Does your firm ensure I'll stand time's test?
Do you pull strings to have each effort picked
by a premier publication? One quick draft
in the condition of a pre-existing sonnet,
and the English-speaking world might dote upon it. . . .
But truth be told, my first attempts aren't craft.
Sonnet Insurance, kindly file this letter;
insure me later, when I write it better.

Taking My Measure

Edvard Munch (1863–1944), Norway

Two dark clouds have shrouded me from birth:
insanity and illness plagued my kin.
A sickly kid, I was often kept in bed.
One sister had been placed in an asylum
and my erratic father raged and prayed.
He gave me little comfort after Mother
died, consumptive (I was barely five):
"She's with God in heaven, watching you,
and grieving every time you misbehave."
At night he'd read us children tales of Poe
and I would waken shaking, imagining
a blade above me swinging to and fro.

My sister Sophie suffered nightmares, too;
we'd swap our horrors over morning porridge.
She always understood my fickle moods
and my need to draw and paint. I was fourteen,
she just one year older, when consumption
stole her energy and then her breath.
I painted her beside her bedside window
where her long, red hair and pallid face
were bathed in winter sun as leitmotif.
Although my father decried art to be
"unholy trade," I found in painting Sophie
a way to lift my soul apart from grief.

Father said real work would steady me,
and packed me off to engineering school.
I did not last. I itched to only paint—
to try to show the ache of isolation,
the bile of envy, the thralls of love and passion,
the palls of shame, anxiety, and dread.
One evening as I strolled, all my senses
went awry. The sky turned red as blood
in fiery swirls above the blue-black fjord—
the piercing scream of nature was a torment,
vast, infinite—my whole body heard it.
I slumped against a railing, dazed and spent.

The critics all dismissed my early work
as "half-done," and called me arrogant.
Becoming estranged from friends and family,
I clung to one, a cousin's wife. In trysts,
she promised she would leave him, but she lied.
Sleeping little and guzzling aquavit,
I had a breakdown, and landed in a clinic.
Eight months of electric shock treatments
calmed me. Healthy foods, herbal baths
and sleeping potions restored my body's health.
The doctor let me keep on working; painting
was the tonic that I prescribed myself.

I moved into a four-square little house
away from tempting women and Oslo bars.
Since then I've lived an ordered life, alone
for all these years—I cannot host a guest,
as anyone might set me off again.
I'm nearing eighty, painting what will be
my last self-portrait. It's rough; its shapes are flat.
I'm in a mismatched suit and shined-up shoes,
standing as if ordered to be here
between my bed and grandfather clock.
That clock has lost its hands and I, as well,
appear blank-faced—the man that time forgot.

I'm weary of this self-absorbed endeavor;
my attic's stacked with seventy self-portraits.
It's been a way for me to take my measure
since *The Scream,* where I embodied terror,
and *Ashes,* where I hid my face in shame.
Now it's mostly landscapes that I paint,
and they sell well enough. But all my paintings
of the past few decades cannot hold
a candle to my fervent early works
that radiate my grief and fear and pain.
Electric treatments calmed my mind; but too,
they dimmed the light that was my precious bane.

Flying

I used to know exactly how to fly,
in dreams. I'd revel in the weightless ease
of springing up into a moonlit sky
and banking shoulders round the crowns of trees.
The gabled roofs below were open books
on chests of sleeping houses; I could rise
and glide, or swoop to revel in the looks
of windows, widened like astonished eyes.

It seemed this power left me till I spent
some time last night once more borne up by air.
But then began a long and slow descent
where all my flapping got me exactly nowhere:
at once a nightmare, ironic lullaby,
and a dream to show me how to die.

The Invaders

"It's small," the doctor says,
"but your cancer is invasive."

    I begin to envision
    a horde of Huns on horseback
    in a thunderous attack.
    Charging archers, wild-eyed,
    pierce the unprotected sides
    of villagers like me who cower
    at the carnage, at the tower
    of smoke above each mountain town.
    One Hun eyes me up and down. . . .

"The cancer has grown beyond
a duct," the doctor continues.
"That's all 'invasive' means."

    At that, invaders pull up reins
    and horses rear and stamp.
    Huns dismount on dusty plains,
    unpack their makeshift camp.
    Will they stay or will they go?
    I wait for history to know.

My Block of Time

> With italicized words from "Our God, Our Help in Ages Past,"
> a Congregational hymn by Isaac Watts, written 1708

Once I could fish in an ocean of free-wheeling time—
each darter a wish, a catch-and-release in unreeling time.

Then time was a warm, wide bay; I paddled and floated
until a shoal around the bend, a perilous feeling of time.

Time, like an ever-rolling stream, bears all its sons away.
They fly forgotten, as a dream, I sing in bell-pealing time.

I'm an ant crawling up the wall. Inches below me increase
as those above me decrease. I'm nearing my ceiling of time.

Breaths may number three quarters of a billion in a lifetime.
What's my number? Air, conspire with me in stealing time!

Now put words aside—go out to smell the fresh-cut grass,
writer. All the gifts of the present are revealing. It's time.

Old Irish Superstitions

If by mistake you put your shirt on inside-out,
you'll have good luck all day, looking like a lout.

It's seven years bad luck if your mirror breaks or cracks;
your shattered soul requires all those years for growing back.

Spilled salt bodes ill. A pinch tossed over your left shoulder,
though, blinds the devil's eyes, and leaves you all the bolder.

A woman brings bad luck to knit at night unless the sheep—
all nearby rams, ewes, and lambs—are known to be asleep.

Itchy nose? A fist fight's coming. Itchy palm? Either way
means money: if the left, you'll get it; if the right, you'll pay.

If you spot a pair of magpies, joy awaits ahead.
Just one bodes ill. Salute it, and you have naught to dread.

If a robin flies inside, a dear one's drawing their last breath.
For a soul's flight to heaven, open a window after death.

When rain at a burial falls like your tears, take heart.
That sympathetic weather is a good-luck counterpart.

Gallarus Oratory

Dingle Peninsula, Ireland

                It's
             like a tent
          that's puffed with
       wind, and like the hull of
      an upturned ship. This chapel
      has withstood a thousand years of
      coastal storms; its stones were cut and
      meshed tight in four gently sloping walls.
      Like a tent, this small-room space sheltered
      monks and travelers on pilgrimage. And like a
    a ship, it took those seekers to an unknown place
    and brought them home once more. I duck my head
    to enter this strange and   tomb-like chapel where
    the near-dark blinds and   holds me still as ancient
    stone. A single window's   tiny arch in the east wall
    beams its narrow light as   if a promise to safeguard.
    I emerge to relish the sun   and to thank the darkness.

Shards of Knowing

> Vojna Memorial, Lešetice, Czech Republic

The guide tells us shards of what she knows
about this former forced labor camp.
"I live nearby. I volunteer, and this
is just my second week," Marta says,
with one hand on her tiny necklace cross.

She gives our tourist group an overview
of how and when the Soviet regime
imprisoned Czechs suspected of dissent.
"For cooks and guards, they hired locals. But,"
she firmly adds, "Soviets ran the camp."

"They forced the men to mine uranium
for bombs, and hundreds died from radiation."
Marta shows us rusted trams on tracks
that carted out the blackened mining waste
into looming mounds beside the fence.

Pointed posts and corner sentry towers
punctuate the lines of thick barbed wire.
Someone asks if prisoners escaped.
"One did," the guide replies, "but seven more
were shot and killed, here or at the border."

There's silence. I ask her softly if she had
a relative imprisoned here. She pauses,
then tells us, "I had a grandfather here
for years. I don't know much about his time.
Let's walk on. The library is next."

That little room is packed with party tracts.
I picture her weary grandfather, more than willing
to sit and read anything at all.
While Marta decries the men's indoctrination,
Stalin scowls down from his prominent frame.

Down some steps and ducking heads to enter,
we cluster next in claustrophobic dark
to hear, "The Hole, the harshest punishment.
Imagine summer heat," Marta murmurs,
"or sleeping on this bare concrete in winter."

We shiver under a steel gray sky while trooping
to a barrack. "Sometimes, to break their minds,"
our guide relates, "the guards forced men to stand
beside their bunks all night. If someone dozed,
the guards would bellow and bang the metal bars."

I almost glimpse a gray-haired sleeper sway
into what was the hospital, a room
with four beds, a cabinet, and one white coat.
"A prisoner was admitted," Marta winces,
"only if he'd lost the strength to walk."

Our guide is looking spent herself. Tour done,
I thank her and she leans her head to mine.
"My *Deda* . . . a barrack guard eleven years . . .
to feed his many children." With that she turns
and takes a step away, her shoulders hunched.

Rain begins to pelt the gravel walk
and I scurry to the bus, the last to board.
Marta smiles with a mock salute.
As the bus pulls away she stands stock-still
and shrinks inside the camp's open gate.

Deda: Czech for grandfather

Garden Wedding

A spate of rain blew through at dawn today;
its sprinkled glints are scattered on the grass
where fresh-faced guests encircle her en masse.
Her vision shaped this artful, bright array
of clustered tables, dahlias in bouquets,
herself an ivory satin willow. The groom,
like steady sun, has loved her into bloom.
Their joy will last long past this blessing day.
And yet, just now, I almost cannot stay.
No twinge of envy from this graying mother,
just my shudder: they'll live so far away.
My daughter's more like me than any other,
or was. I hold my husk of grief inside.
This rite entwines, and too, it will divide.

Since My Father's Death

His ethnic slurs, I will not speak about,
nor how he'd quell dissension with his roar.
Erupting in a jeer or angry shout,
those reprimands would chill me to the core.
He called to bawl my history teacher out,
"Why do you teach these students to abhor
America's internment camps?" He'd spout,
and I would cringe but couldn't risk a war;
against that foe, I'd never win.
                                But now,
as if his heart by death has been restored,
I sense his presence wishing to avow
more love and far less venom than before.
Somehow I know *his* spirit once was broken.
Somehow I hear the words he left unspoken.

Icons

> Kehinde Wiley, b.1977, United States

This artist saw how whites were lining walls
of art museums and pages of art books.
To open minds and widen hallowed halls,
he paints the same ennobled, prideful looks
in epic scale on people black or brown
like him. He makes them vibrant, rich with power—
the mother in a sweeping Gucci gown;
the boy with hands that pray but eyes that glower;
the girl a goddess with coiled crown of hair;
the man enrobed as Emperor victorious;
the President who's poised in natural flair.
Each looks secure in strength and station glorious.
His portraits, bridging Harlem and Versailles,
tread uneasy ground, both truth and lie.

Guided Hike at the Volcano

Mt. Arenal, La Fortuna, Costa Rica

We meet the guide, José; he's short and slim,
in shirt and slacks that match his light brown skin
like camouflage. He knows, by sound and eye,
the motmots, toucans, and barbets flapping by.
He names the epiphytes—the mosses, vines
and ferns that coat the trees in lush designs;
we, too, feel wrapped in earthy greens. He lifts
one hand for silence, and our attention shifts:
it sounds to us like distant thunder rumbling.
"That's the music of the mountain, the tumbling
of boulders from the mouth of Arenal,"
José says, eyes closed. Our voices fall
to murmurs after that, and we stop to hear
new rumbles with frissons of gleeful fear.

We follow him like acolytes in church.
Partway up the mountain on a perch,
our group is frozen in a double-take—
agog to gaze upon the cobalt lake
below, the emerald fields in sunbeams' glow,
the western clouds backlit by peach and rose.
High above, the cone sends plumes of smolder
as it spews each distant crashing boulder.
When they bounce, they spark an orange wake
in dusky air—what fireworks they make!
José looks anxious. "We must go," he calls.
"It's late, and darkness in the tropics falls
fast." But we're transfixed. We contemplate
this world around us in its primal state.
Standing on this ledge we're celebrants

of air, earth, and water elements—
and fire in each fearsome boulder's glow.
At last, resignedly, we turn to go.
The guide leads us through the dark with care,
his flashlight—and perhaps his silent prayer.

Namaste

    Sanskrit: *I bow to you*

From the window of the tourist bus
snarled in Casablanca traffic,
I gazed at a wizened man
in white robe and turban,
his face chestnut brown.
When he looked up
our eyes met.
My palms
rose,
as if
in prayer—
which startled me
but perhaps not him:
likewise he lifted palms,
pressed them lightly at his chest
while regarding me through the glass
with wrinkled, warm, penetrating eyes.

Bring no harm to the trees . . .

> *nor burn them with fire, especially those which are fruitful.*
> —Abu Bakr, first Muslim caliph (632 to 634 C.E.),
> in his wartime rules for soldiers in Mecca. Though he was
> fond of poetry, the words that follow are imagined.

"Bring no harm to date palm trees," he could
have continued to his men. "Our people use
each part by the fruit, the oil to burn, the wood
to build our boats that ply the Sea of Aden.
We plait the sturdy leaves to make our shoes
and hats, our roofing thatch, our garden baskets.
Christians used the fronds to line the roads
of Jerusalem for Jesus. They're laden
on *Sukkot* huts by Jews, and they wrap caskets
for all of us, our bodies' last abodes.
So take from date palms only what you need;
this tree provides for every tribe and creed.

"Don't harm a pomegranate tree," he might
go on. "Juicy seeds can quench in fall
when other trees are bare. Each tart-sweet bite
proclaims its name, the Fruit of Paradise.
And yet this fruit's a stern, symbolic call
to Jewish people for each coming year:
perform good deeds prolific as its seeds.
Blood-red, it stands for Christian sacrifice,
when Jesus knew his death was drawing near."
Abu might have slowed his speech to plead,
"Savor the pomegranate tree's rewards,
and cut its crimson gift with gentle swords.

"And bring no harm to one more tree so good,
the sycamore fig—its spreading canopy
a host who shares his tent, a cooling hood.
Lean back on its smooth bark to relish fruit
and breathe its fragrant leaves. A panoply,
this Tree of Life! So too for Amos, a prophet
of Judea and picker of sycamore figs,
a nomad while his faith was seeking root.
My speech is done, my men. Now do not scoff at
my last words: I wave these fig tree sprigs
for prophet Amos, who lived to praise his Lord;
Allah is not the only name adored!"

The men began their trek to war. They spared
the dusty trees, and only paused to ease
their hunger with juicy fruits the branches shared.
Exhausted, hot, on sore and blistered feet,
they came upon a grove of jasmine trees
with fragrant boughs of ivory blossoms. Above
their heads, as men reclined and dozed in heat,
petals drifted down on them like neighbors
welcoming the tribe with wordless love.
When soldiers woke they took up unused sabers,
set them down beside a nearby plow,
and turned for home, as dreams—and gods—allow.

Paradise Leased

The newborn smiles, cradled in your arms,
while lilacs scent the balmy air of May.
But fits of colic dim the infant's charms,
the fall will shrivel every fragrant flower,
and pristine snowbanks sully into ember.
Still, there comes a day or just an hour,
whether in July or dark December,
when a jolt of joy can take your breath away.
Your senses quiver, as if a gust of grace
had flown you to nirvana. It will flit—
that evanescent moment will erase
any hope of ownership. Just visit
this marvelous abode and be content,
as paradise is only yours to rent.

March 21st

Chasing measured clarity,
I work, obsess, despair, give up—
not like the springtime world, in vernal

balance. If I possessed internal
equanimity, I'd keep
a steady state like equinox.

I shouldn't overlook the shocks
that bracket equal day and night—
fires, quakes, and hurricanes.

Through all, resilient Earth maintains
its equilibrium, with time
and mystery of unknown sense.

The spring will play in plot and sequence—
snowdrop, crocus, rose, and lily—
allotted spaces, days to flower.

Winter doesn't dint their power;
it allows it. Constant blooming
would fracture greater symmetry.

Daily roses would limit me,
as well. I'll trust in wider arcs
that balance into parity.

Spiral

Is this some neural outgrowth of my soul,
the shifting current coursing down from brain
to heart? It's like a channel bell that tolls
both ode to joy and dirge for dark night's pain,
this sudden shiver linking mind and spine.
We hold our little granddaughter at the shore;
she's spellbound by the terns at waterline
and swells that tumble down the beach with roars.
We find a conch whose rosy throat retells
the ancient lore of surf-and-heartbeat echo
when spiral ear is pressed to spiral shell,
a parallel and mystery. All I know
is wrapped inside my arms right now, swirled
in spiral arms of stars that gird the world.

The Resplendent Quetzal

    a bird species in Monteverde, Costa Rica

In flaming red, sapphire, and emerald green,
their feathers glow with iridescent sheen,
    like sunlit leaves still wet
from recent rain. A female stands between
two males who whistle, swoop, and preen,
    competing in duet.

The blue plume feathers in each suitor's tail,
dazzling in the light, seem out of scale
    to bodies half that long.
In treetop breeze these feathers waft and sail—
two mythic ocean creatures' fishtails
    plying liquid air with song.

Gods of the Air, ancient peoples called
them. But Mayans and Aztecs would be appalled:
    these Gods are rare today,
as our dominion in this land has sprawled.
Beneath the birds I hold my breath, enthralled,
    before they glide away.

Naming the Sacred

> "But the angel of YHWH said to him, 'Why
> do you ask my name? It is beyond understanding.'"
> —Judges 13:18, King James Bible

Old Hebraic YHWH translated into Greek
was unpronounceable, and over time became
Yahweh, a name for God no reverent Jew would speak.

Though Christians may insist upon a proper name
like Father (lest God be thought a metaphor), the spark
of Inward Light is the image Quakers claim—

divinity in each of us. Just now, in the dark,
a meteor has arced its echo past my eye,
like the landing on the wire of the lark

who puffs its yellow breast against an ashen sky
and wings away. In underbrush of tangled green,
I've never seen (although devotedly I try)

the Hermit Thrush. He whistles out in serpentine
minor notes—a sweet but melancholy voice
entwining joys and sorrows behind his verdant screen.

At natural wonders seen and felt, I rejoice.
I've chanced upon another metaphor, a sign
that can't be spelled or spoken: my keyboard choice

of <^>, three pointed abstract symbols that align
into this partial star or angel incomplete.
It's all that I will ever know of grand design.

About the Author

After graduating from Skidmore College as a Studio Art major, Barbara Lydecker Crane worked as a graphic designer and then a professional quilt artist. Her landscape quilts hang on corporate, hospital, museum, and private collection walls. About twenty years ago, she turned to writing poetry. In 2007 she joined the Powow River Poets in Newburyport, MA, and to date she has published upwards of 300 poems in journals and anthologies. In addition to poetry and art, Barb loves to travel. She lives near Boston with her husband; they have two daughters, two sons-in-law, four grandchildren, and—for good measure—two granddogs.

www.ingramcontent.com/pod-product-compliance
Lightning Source LLC
Chambersburg PA
CBHW071011160426
43193CB00012B/2001